For Pauline Neal —

With grateful appreciation
and all good wishes

Gloria Hirsch

THE ART OF JUDGING AND EXHIBITING
Flower Arrangements

Sylvia Hirsch

THE ART

FLOWER

BY THE AUTHOR

The Art of Table Setting and Flower Arrangement
The Art of Judging and Exhibiting Flower Arrangements

OF JUDGING

AND EXHIBITING

ARRANGEMENTS

Thomas Y. Crowell Company

ESTABLISHED 1834

New York

TO MY COLLEAGUES
the dedicated teachers and judges who
have raised flower arranging to an art

Acknowledgments

M Y DEEPEST appreciation goes to countless unsung friends and colleagues whose steadfast constancy inspired me to complete this book. In particular, Margaret Cochrane Cole, Mae Cronin, Elizabeth Edmondson, Irene Frank, and Wynn Hescock.

I would like to thank the following exhibitors for providing me with photographs of their distinguished work: Mrs. Edward Ascher, Mrs. Edward H. Bergles, Mrs. Edwin B. Dean, Mrs. James E. Flynn, Mrs. Elmer Grimmett, Mrs. William R. King, and Mrs. Donald L. Stevens.

To the following gentlemen a word of thanks for generously providing material I have used in some of my arrangements: John Diegnan, George Johnson, and James Stotter.

To the expert judges who so conscientiously served with me at the Latham Flower Show School and the Boston Flower Show, my devoted thanks—Mrs. Willard L. Fitzpatrick, Mrs. Donald L. Millham, Mrs. Raymond C. Cronin, and Mrs. Howard H. Rubin.

I am ever grateful to Eleanor Mamorsky for her devoted friendship and invaluable assistance always.

And to the members of the Thomas Y. Crowell staff who have been so helpful in all phases of this book, I am so grateful.

SYLVIA HIRSCH

Contents

Goals and Challenges

FLOWER arrangers and judges of flower shows agree that a better understanding of and a fresh approach to the practices of judging are greatly needed.

We aim to arrive at a broader common denominator that will raise the basic standards of flower arranging and permit greater flexibility in exhibiting and judging.

We desire to encourage freedom of expression for judges and exhibitors—while continuing to maintain an awareness of the fundamental principles of art.

These are the goals of the judges' schools, judges' councils, and all forward-thinking judges and creative exhibitors.

RAISING STANDARDS

Some judges would still like to see judging a mathematical procedure as precise as the workings of an IBM machine. For them it would be a matter of defining right and wrong, with no deviations allowed. Be cautious of that shortsighted, narrow-minded attitude.

Rules take form because those with experience have found them to be the best, most logical solutions to the problems at hand. Rules are helpful to novices and judges who feel more confident in being able to refer to them. They serve a definite and constructive purpose *up to a point*. Use them, follow them, be guided by them, but in creative work don't let them hamper your originality and interpretation.

Obviously, some rules in flower show work are necessary. They tend to standardize procedure and produce a common ground of understanding. They are a prescribed guide to proper and fair analysis. The schedule, a résumé of the theme, class, and requirements for the flower show, defines the assignment for the exhibitor. It also aids the judge in analyzing, understanding, interpreting, and appraising how well the exhibitor has fulfilled the assignment.

The current National Council rules are the result of the best understanding of conditions at a particular time. As times, tastes, and styles change, the National Council has felt—and may again feel—the need to adjust some of the present regulations.

ENCOURAGE EXHIBITORS

Because rules are guideposts they should be used as such. They are not meant to curtail individual expression but to inspire and guide the exhibitor and judge. If there are too many rules, or if they are overemphasized or confining, the exhibitor's imagination may become constricted and stultified. Consequently, the end result could be completely uninspired, though perhaps technically "correct."

Often a judge bound by literal rules frequently overlooks the inspirational qualities of an exhibit while dwelling on minor technical imperfections. Thus she loses sight of its over-all *spirit, originality,* and *beauty.*

Fortunately as soon as a rule becomes set procedure, someone with imagination and a desire for freer expression may successfully disprove it by presenting a contradictory, though nevertheless satisfactory, exception. Thus she underlines the truth that creative talent and flexibility are essential in making or breaking rules.

Flower arranging, one of the loveliest of the creative arts, must not be confined by the rigidity of inflexible rules, any more than painting, sculpture, or music. The judge must keep alert and open-minded for the unfamiliar and the original—for the exception that

THE FUTURE LOOK *Ultra-restrained use of plant material: white ash twigs (Fraxinus americana), tritoma, and tree ivy (Fatshedera lizei). Composition is an understated complement to the unique bronze sculpture by Lipman-Wulf.* Arranger: Mrs. James C. Flynn. *(Photo: W. W. Hennessy)*

may prove the rule—provided it does not violate the requirements of the schedule. Give due credit and recognition to the exhibitor who has artistic courage.

Even though judges differ about certain points, the exhibitor, whether an award winner or not, should gain much from the judges' constructive, unbiased evaluations. The award is not what really counts. It is what we have learned from the experience and the judges' helpful comments that makes competition healthy, educational, and inspirational.

EXPANDING HORIZONS

There are some flower show judges who would still impose conformity and orthodoxy in teaching and thinking. This is not in keeping with today's freedom of expression. As judges, teachers,

HOSANNA *An original expressive composition displaying avant-garde design. The selection and skillful handling of all elements is superb in this study in black and red against gold.* Arranger: Mrs. Donald L. Stevens. *(Photo: Commonwealth Photographers, Inc.)*

and creative artists we must keep open-minded and up-to-date with our rapidly changing times.

Our creative field is almost limitless. Every day we find new ways for individual self-expression in flower arranging. These creative experiments, though sometimes strange, must be respected, encouraged, and cultivated.

TESTED BASIC PRINCIPLES

Imagination and open-mindedness are facets of the creative process that result in new ideas and new presentations. On the other hand—and this is very important—tested principles are still basic; they help us to maintain our balance as we move ahead. All art requires a look at the past.

Tested principles have endured because they reflect the realities of our world, the realities of continuity and change. We are now in the midst of an upheaval in the world of art. Although we fan our imaginations for excitement and stimulation we should maintain our artistic equilibrium. This we learn through flower show exhibiting and judging.

Judging can be fun even though it is a sobering and serious business. It is a complex and controversial phase of a most satisfying and stimulating creative art. Conscientious as we may be, we should maintain our perspective and our sense of humor, attributes which will enable us to see things in their true light. If we view objectively we can fully appreciate the beauty, spirit, and intent of the exhibitor and enjoy the excitement of our task.

HIGHLIGHTS!

—A fresh approach to judging is needed.
—We must broaden our goals:

(1) Encourage freedom of expression
(2) Raise basic standards
(3) Expand our artistic horizons

—Let rules be your guide, don't let them rule you absolutely. Be flexible.

LEAN AND LINEAR *Dried okra creates a strong effective structural line. A graceful pod (royal poinciana) encloses space, which balances the interesting green-bronze kalanchoë and blue-red ginger blossom.* Arranger: the author. (*Photo:* The Miami Herald)

CHAPTER 2

Connoisseur or Critic?

Deliberate with caution, but act with decision; yield with graciousness, or oppose with firmness.

C. C. COLTON

TO JUDGE means to evaluate, appreciate, review. It also means to give criticism (always constructive), to give an opinion, to arrive at a decision, to award a verdict.

QUALITIES OF A GOOD JUDGE

To be a competent judge, a comprehensive knowledge of the subject is necessary. It is generally attained through study and application and exposure to allied arts. In the case of flower arrangements and table settings the following are essential:

1 A knowledge of the principles of design and their practical use.

2 An understanding of color—theoretically, technically, and artistically.

3 An ability to recognize plant material—its suitability and its potential in the individual arrangement.

4 An appreciation of the intent of the exhibitor and a willingness to understand and credit the inspiration behind each arrange-

ment. Being a skilled exhibitor oneself will make the judge more aware of the problems involved.

5 A complete comprehension of the schedule. This is attained by careful preparatory study and analysis sometime prior to the show, and then again before starting to judge. Too many times points of importance are overlooked because the schedule is read too casually.

6 The ability to stay clear-minded, concentrated, and relaxed. (Comfortable shoes are essential for long hours of standing.)

7 An acquaintance with related arts and a desire for an increased knowledge of them.

THE IDEAL JUDGE

In addition to practical and technical knowledge of the subject, certain native qualities make the difference between an ordinary judge and a superior one. They are: sensitivity, insight, understanding, kindness, consistency, logic, stability, objectivity, open-

INSPIRED BY NATURE *Exotic plant material and hand-finished driftwood container appear to have a natural affinity for one another. Amaryllis, cut philodendron leaves and tendrils.* Arranger: the author. *(Photo: William Sevecke)*

mindedness; and tact, long experience, and the ability to impart evaluations simply and directly.

Obviously personalities, personal likes, or unfortunate personal experiences should not enter into or be reflected in making decisions. There is no room for prejudice if one is to be a conscientious, capable judge.

Judges create an attitude of authority. This will impress others and give you confidence. Pedantic, dogmatic, self-satisfied judges are generally people of limited vision and learning.

Ideally, every judge and exhibitor should feel the responsibility for keeping up-to-date and informed. Pity the poor, highly creative exhibitor whose work is to be judged by someone whose standards are passé. How important it is that both judge and exhibitor be alert—aware of new trends in their own and allied fields.

What is the best way to accomplish this? Take advantage of every opportunity. Read—read all you can in your own and related fields. Keep current with the latest rules in *National Gardener*. Attend judges' schools, judges' council meetings, and lectures; participate in flower shows; visit museums and art galleries; observe new fashions; enjoy nature and become familiar with its bounties. Read —study—participate—enjoy.

OBJECTIVE JUDGING

Judging is as good or as poor as the judge. That is why informed, well-trained, and experienced judges are essential to the growth of the art of flower arranging. Though knowledge, training, and experience are basic in appraising and evaluating, a judge should be constantly aware that other desirable traits contribute in part to an honest, objective decision.

As most of us mature, we establish certain standards. These become unconscious reactions and thus can indeed influence us. Decisions may be colored by personal biases, such as partiality to a particular color or style. Therefore, it is important for judges to be aware of their inner responses and to train themselves to be objective. In new classes emphasizing creativity, however, the judge may become involved, and in fact should become involved, in order to appreciate the artistic intent of the exhibitor.

STYLE AND SOPHISTICATION *Ingeniously contrived pedestal in iridescent violet combines a newel post with sculptured wood. Unusual colors (green, orange, violet) keynote the composition of pineapple leaves, lilies, and croton foliage.* Arranger: the author. *(Photo:* The Miami Herald)

CRITIC'S CHOICE *Distinctive plant material frames and echoes the classic posture of the mahogany figure. Scolopendrium, holly fern, pothos, clivia, and grape branch.* Arranger: the author. *(Photo: William Sevecke)*

RESPONSIBILITY OF A JUDGE

Judging, whether in courts of law or in appraising art, is a great responsibility. Though one sphere may be more serious than the other, each has a code of ethics, and the basic premises are not unlike.

A judge should be able to compare facts and ideas, to comprehend their significance and thus distinguish truth from falsehood, right from wrong. The judge should be both connoisseur and critic. A *critic* is one who has knowledge and experience sufficient to decide on the merits of a question; a *connoisseur* is one who has an appetite for knowledge and a versatile mind.

Judges, even the most capable ones, may not—and frequently do not—entirely agree on every point. The differences in opinion reflect the human element—the intelligence, the cultural background, the emotional stability, the sense of humor, and the experience of the judge.

It is good to be courageous, firm, and gracious. It is important to believe in yourself. If you feel you are right, be sure you have arrived at your decision after *cautious deliberation*. Do not be dogmatic. Seek to be constructive in your analysis, rather than just try to please. Above all, remember that the majority decision of the judges is final.

We as judges must never lose sight of the fact that a flower show judge is very much an artist in her own right. Through greater knowledge, deeper understanding, and tolerance for the unfamiliar, she has it in her power to make a major contribution to the art of flower arranging. Above all she alone can help to create an accepting atmosphere in which accomplished arrangers and newcomers to the field can confidently develop their own individual contributions to this lively and satisfying art.

HIGHLIGHTS!

—A judge is both connoisseur and critic. "To judge" means to
    know, to appreciate, to appraise objectively.
—Qualities of a good judge are:

CLASSIC SERENITY *Striking forms, rhythmic placement, and craftsmanlike assembling creates a dramatic setting for this portrait in green-bronze. Cycas palm, cacti, velvet anthurium, accented by calla lilies.* Arranger: *the author,* (Photo: *William Sevecke*)

(1) knowledge of design
(2) understanding of color
(3) an affinity for nature
(4) appreciation of exhibitor's intent
(5) comprehension of schedule
(6) an alert mind and a relaxed manner
(7) an acquaintance with related arts.

—Attributes of an ideal judge are:

(1) sensitivity
(2) consistency
(3) objectivity
(4) tact
(5) long experience
(6) the power to transmit evaluations simply and directly.

—A capable judge knows her responsibilities and makes her contribution to her art through knowledge, understanding, and tolerance.

CHAPTER 3

The Delicate Art of Judging

BECAUSE being a judge involves a moral responsibility to oneself and to the exhibitors, it is important for the judge to be true to her ideals and beliefs. She must see what she judges and judge what she sees. She must not be swayed by what she expects or wishes to find but must concentrate on facts and be moved only by imaginative interpretation. Under no circumstances does a judge ever handle or readjust an exhibit. She judges it as it stands. In other words, though judging is an appreciative art, it must be approached objectively, with intelligence and sensitivity.

Of all the aspects of flower show work, judging is probably the most harassing and controversial, though it is without doubt one of the most challenging and interesting. Even though there are rules—established art principles and certain guidelines set down for us by the National Council—there is still wide latitude permitted, so that the judge and the exhibitor may use their imagination and individuality. This attitude must be encouraged if the art of flower arranging is to continue to progress.

THE SCHEDULE

The schedule is the story and the law of the show. Established by the schedule committee of a flower show, it gives a résumé of the theme, classes, rules, and regulations governing the show.

Here is a partial schedule for the artistic section of a flower show demonstrating the correlation in the theme of the show, titles of classes, and their descriptions.

NEW HORIZONS

SECTION A: EXPRESSIVE OF TODAY

Class 1: Carte Blanche
An abstract or free-form arrangement staged on a pedestal 24 inches square, 40 inches from the floor.

Class 2: Design Experiment
Interpretation of a work of art by a modern artist (to be incorporated into the exhibit). Staged in a module 3 feet wide by 5 feet high.

Class 3: Science Moves Ahead
A geometric or abstract design.

SECTION B: CONTEMPORARY DINING

Class 4: Gracious Dining in the Contemporary Manner
Luncheon table setting. Functional type. Four place settings. Table: 30 inches wide, 60 inches long.

Class 5: The Old Order Changeth
A functional buffet in a contemporary spirit. Service for four. Table: 36 inches wide, 72 inches long.

Class 6: Ultra Smart
An exhibition capsule setting, displayed against a background table covering, one plate, napkin, glass or cup and saucer, accessary(ies), and decorative unit. (Background: 36 inches high, 28 inches wide, 24 inches deep.)

RULES AND REGULATIONS

Some fresh plant material must be used in all exhibits. Fresh plant material must predominate in the floral composition in classes four, five, and six.

There are no restrictions in classes one, two, and three, except that some fresh plant material must be used. *Note:* The committee should state the size, type, and location of tables, dimensions of background, and number of place settings. Other requirements and limitations must be stated in the rules; for example, the kind of plant material and type of table, whether functional or exhibition.

PROBLEMS AND SOLUTIONS

Most problems in exhibiting and judging arise because schedules, including the rules, are ambiguous, incomplete, or uninspired. A schedule, in addition to being timely and interesting, should state all requirements and provide full explanations appropriate for the *current show*. Sometimes rules and regulations are lifted in entirety from old schedules with no reference to the new schedule. This occurs all too frequently, causing a great deal of difficulty.

Often, specified plant material is not available. This can result in bare spots in the exhibit that will disturb the staging.

A schedule should be clear, concise, and consistent. There should be a close relationship between the wording used to describe the assignment, the title of class, and the theme of the show.

Exhibitors and judges are happier with a limited number of restrictions or requirements, because too many requirements confine their efforts. Schedules that are written simply and explicitly, that show vision and allow freedom, have the greatest appeal. They bring forth the largest number of exhibitors and generally make for the most attractive shows. Above all, they facilitate judging and make the judges' decisions more understandable and logical.

To write a schedule you must first decide upon a theme. Make sure it is broad, inspiring, timely. Relate your classes to your chosen theme, so that there is continuity throughout. Each class should be fully descriptive, with all requirements and rules spelled out.

THEMES TO STIMULATE YOUR SCHEDULE PLANNING

Themes are the broader general headings. *Class titles and requisites* develop from the theme. The following lists should not be followed dogmatically but should serve to spur your creativity. In them, classes are correlated with the themes and tabulated in charts with cross reference for your convenience.

This is just a beginning. Spaces are left in which you may—and should—enter your own titles for themes and classes. The possibilities are unlimited. Let your imagination soar.

ODE TO THE TROPICS *Exotic natural plant materials vitalize a well-crafted composition in a range of colors from green to chartreuse to pale yellow, from rosy pink to orange-red. Palm boots, ti leaves, draecena foliage, wood roses, baby green bananas, akee, kumquats, carambola, and sweet gum balls.* Arranger: Mrs. Edwin B. Dean.

FLOWER SHOW THEMES AND CLASSES
WITH UNLIMITED POSSIBILITIES

(ARTISTIC DIVISION)

---

1   NEW HORIZONS
     THOUGHTS OF TOMORROW

---

2   CONTEMPORARY LIVING
     OUR WAY OF LIFE

---

3   THE AMERICAN STORY
     GREAT MOMENTS IN HISTORY

---

4   EXPLORING ART
     HOMAGE TO BEAUTY

---

5   SALUTE TO THE UNITED NATIONS
     WORLDS TO EXPLORE

---

6   WE WOMEN
     OUR TOWN

---

7   WOMEN OF THE BIBLE
     MYTH AND RITUAL

---

8   MY FAVORITE THINGS
     FOOD FOR THOUGHT

FLOWER SHOW CLASSES—KEYED TO SUGGESTED FLOWER SHOW THEMES

CONTEMPORARY AND AVANT-GARDE

	1	2	3	4	5	6	7	8
Swiftness of Things	✓	✓	✓		✓			
Supersonic Experiment	✓		✓	✓				
Foreshadows of the Future	✓			✓				
Shadows and Space	✓			✓			✓	
Sound and Light	✓			✓	✓		✓	
Automation versus Nature	✓			✓				
Hope of the Future	✓	✓		✓	✓			
Lean and Linear	✓			✓				
Rhythm and Accent	✓	✓		✓		✓		
Expectations	✓			✓	✓			
Science Ahead	✓	✓	✓					

INTERPRETIVE: FREE AND INSPIRING

	1	2	3	4	5	6	7	8
Inspired by the Dance				✓		✓	✓	✓
Performing Arts		✓	✓	✓		✓	✓	✓
Our Galleries	✓		✓	✓				
The Museum World	✓		✓	✓	✓			✓
Mixed Media		✓		✓		✓		
Memorabilia			✓	✓				

Interpretive: Free and Inspiring (Continued)

	1	2	3	4	5	6	7	8
Echoes of Spain—Reign in Spain					✓			✓
Influenced by the Far East		✓		✓	✓		✓	
Sports	✓	✓	✓					✓
Books on Review		✓	✓				✓	✓
Colonial Heritage			✓			✓		✓
Our National Parks—Majestic Arrangement Incorporating One of Nature's Artifacts	✓		✓					✓
Collector's Choice			✓	✓				✓

COLOR IMAGES

	1	2	3	4	5	6	7	8
Autumn Harmonies		✓		✓		✓		✓
Spring Yellow		✓		✓		✓	✓	✓
The Orient Speaks			✓	✓	✓		✓	✓
Winter's Tale	✓	✓				✓	✓	
Subdued Splendor		✓		✓			✓	
White and Walnut	✓	✓	✓					
Charcoal and Curry	✓	✓	✓					
Happiness Is		✓			✓			✓

DINING TABLES: EVERYDAY—SPECIAL OCCASIONS*

	1	2	3	4	5	6	7	8
Thanksgiving Bounty—a Family Dinner		✓	✓			✓		✓
Harvest Splendor—Buffet		✓	✓			✓		✓
In the Springtime, the Only Pretty Ring Time—Luncheon		✓				✓		✓
Xmas All Aglow—a Family Dinner		✓	✓			✓	✓	✓
Tea for the Bride-to-be	✓	✓				✓		✓
Relaxed Entertaining—Patio Buffet	✓	✓				✓		
Fashion Dictates—Fall Coordinates Spring Ensemble (Functional Capsule Setting)	✓	✓			✓	✓		✓
A Bachelor Entertains (Functional Capsule Setting)	✓	✓			✓			✓
With Style and Sophistication (Exhibition Capsule Setting)	✓	✓		✓		✓		
Crystal Gazing—Luncheon	✓	✓		✓		✓		

* See rules and regulations for number of settings and size of table.

VALUE OF POINT SCORING

Point scoring is a matter of appraising. If a proper scale of points is established and made available in advance of the show, it is an aid to students and to inexperienced judges. It also is valuable to experienced judges, particularly in cases of close competition. The public too can appreciate the assignment more intelligently if a scale of points is designated.

In judging competitive exhibts in flower shows, certain fixed elements and principles must be considered along with such intangibles as interpretation, originality, and distinction.

Experienced judges do not point score each arrangement. They first appraise the class carefully. Each exhibit is mentally evaluated against perfection (100 per cent). Those that fall short are eliminated after due consideration and the remaining exhibits are scored for final decision.

As we view an exhibit, some responses are momentary, other reactions the result of study and analysis. First impressions are strong. However, conscientious analysis may weaken rather than retain their exhilarating effect. Careful study, distance from the exhibit, differences in lighting and perspective can alter the viewer's impressions. So often upon entering a flower show we are impressed by a striking arrangement. After studying it in relation to the schedule (theme, class, and scale of points), however, it sometimes falls short in interpretation, conformity, or execution. If, on the other hand, the exhibit survives both favorably—the first impression and the final analysis—then it undoubtedly has merit.

First a judge should enjoy an arrangement spontaneously. What feelings does it evoke? Excitement, joy, beauty, quiet, nostalgia? Is it stimulating or disturbing? An arrangement should be experienced as a whole, not in parts, to be enjoyed.

The second step is to review and evaluate. A composition is made up of many parts which serve to interpret the ideas and feelings of the artist. When these elements are well chosen and organized according to principles of good design, the composition has meaning. The expression begins with the intent (idea) of the exhibitor, and it develops as her inner feelings guide her in the selection of materials and the placement and organization of them. Hopefully, the result gives expression to her original idea.

An appropriate scale of points is an aid to arriving at, as nearly as possible, a fair and just verdict. It is a control that keeps one from placing undue emphasis on a fault or a virtue.

Should judges ever be uncertain about a minor technicality, they should err on the side of leniency and not penalize the ex-

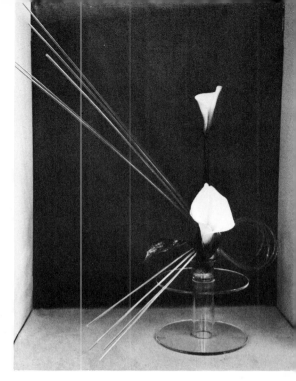

DESIGN EXPERIMENT *Imaginative idea and execution evoke a novel and scintillating feeling. Materials are set in a lucite container designed by the exhibitor. Calla lilies, chinese evergreen foliage, plastic rods against a silver-blue velvet background.* Arranger: Mrs. Elmer Grimmet. *(Photo: Alwood Harvey)*

hibitor unduly. Should they detect a slight flaw or irregularity that does not detract from the over-all beauty of the exhibit, they should not stress it or penalize it disproportionately. The deviation could be called to the attention of the exhibitor by helpful, constructive comments.

STANDARD SYSTEM OF POINT SCORING

There are several systems of point scoring. The one recommended by the National Council of State Garden Clubs in their *Handbook for Flower Shows* is called the standard system. This system is used in all garden clubs in which a standard flower show is the goal.

In the standard system of point scoring, each quality has a perfection mark. Exhibits are measured (evaluated) against that ideal, and the resulting figures are added to make the final score.

In this system there can be only one first, one second, and one third. There may be several honorable mentions, however, if the class is good. If the class is poor, one or more awards may be withheld.

According to this system: A blue ribbon—first—must score 90 or more; a red ribbon—second—must score 85 or more; a yellow ribbon—third—must score 75 or more; a white ribbon—honorable mention—may be awarded to an exhibit when the judges find it has commendable features, even if it falls below the 75 point mark, but it should score 65 or more.

If the top exhibit in the class fails to reach 90, a blue ribbon is not awarded. If the highest score is 88, the top award would be a red ribbon. In cases where a class is of exceptionally high caliber and several exhibits rate in the 90's, e.g., 95, 93, 90, the awards would be designated as first, second, and third, even though all exhibits scored over 90.

Tri-Color, Award of Distinction, and Award of Creativity are the most coveted awards that can be presented in a large, eminently praiseworthy flower show. One, two, or all three awards may be presented if the sections, number of classes, and number of exhibits comply with National Council requirements and if the highest scoring exhibit in the section scores 95 or more.

Scales of points and other specifications for judging standard flower shows (district and state shows) can be found in the National Council of State Garden Clubs' *Handbook for Flower Shows* and subsequent directives and in *The Art of Table Setting and Flower Arrangement* by the author.

POINT SCORING GUIDE

Here are some categories that you may find in your scales of points, as well as qualities to look for under each of the following categories. (These expressions apply to flower arrangement and table setting classes.)

Category	Qualities
Over-all design	Balance (visual); proportion; scale (consistent interrelationship of all elements); rhythm; dominance and contrast.
Distinction and/or originality	Superiority, decided difference, expert craftsmanship; new idea, use of unusual materials and color harmonies; clever use of the usual; smartness, style, good taste.
Compatibility of all materials	Relationship of textures, color harmonies, spirit, over-all unity.
Perfection of decorative unit (used for table setting classes)	All principles of good design apply. Decorative unit(s) should be related in color, texture, and/or spirit. Close correlation to over-all table setting is essential.
Interpretation or conformity to schedule; suitability to occasion	Spirit—adherence to theme, apppropriateness, functionalism.
Personal expression	Original concept—individual style, clarity of purpose, daring.
Color	Conformance to specific color harmony (if requested), use of color (rhythm and balance, relationship to other colors) contrast and interest by use of a variety of textures, forms, and lighting.
Condition—fastidiousness	Freshness, crispness, neatness of plant material, meticulousness of equipment (containers, accessories, background) and appointments (their precision in placement and over-all fastidiousness). (*Note:* When condition is not listed as one of the categories, it should be considered under distinction and/or design.)

SYMBOLS OF PROGRESS *Inventive and and affirmative expression is shown. Bold forms and strong structural outline reflect the modern mood. Wrought iron sculpture, created by the artist, holds extremely unusual plant material: white strelitzia, schefflera, and one croton leaf.* Arranger: the author. *(Photo: William Sevecke)*

Certain categories are included in *every* scale of points, but some are omitted or included to emphasize specific requirements. For example, in a color class, or in a class that emphasizes it, *color, its conformity to schedule and its use* is an essential category, whereas in a creative class, an interpretive class, or a decorative design class, where color is not specificially mentioned in the scale of points, its effective use may be referred to under any of the following: distinction, compatibility, interpretation, or personal expression.

SUGGESTED SCALES OF POINTS
HIGHLIGHTING SPECIAL FEATURES

(The scale of points may be adjusted to suit the specific class.)

"A Little Different." A smart *exhibition capsule* setting to be staged against a background approximately 38 inches high by 30 inches wide by 26 inches deep. Table covering, one plate,

NATURE'S HEIRLOOM *Jaunty lilac branches and a splash of andromeda blossoms spring lifelike from a gnarled old driftwood root. Frosty white carnations accent the graceful line of the budding lilac in this fragrant and dramatic arrangement, designed in homage to spring.* Arranger: the author.

SCIENCE AHEAD *In this inventive composition, pandamus, anthurium, and dieffenbachia foliage, scolopendrium and red amaryllis are combined in a crystal bowl. The formula and accessories deftly interpret the scientific trend.* Arranger: the author. *(Photo: George J. Hirsch)*

napkin, cup and saucer or glass, flower arrangement, and appropriate accessories if desired. Fresh plant material must predominate in decorative unit(s).

QUALITIES BEING SCORED	SCORE NO. 1	SCORE NO. 2
Over-all design	30	25
Distinction and/or originality	20	25
Compatibility of all materials	15	15
Perfection of decorative unit(s)	20	20
Conformity to schedule and/or interpretation	5	10
Condition—fastidiousness	10	5
Total	100	100

"Designed for Today's Living." A *functional* buffet to be set for four. Fresh plant material must predominate in the decorative unit(s). Table: 40 inches by 72 inches.

QUALITIES BEING SCORED	SCORE NO. 1	SCORE NO. 2
Over-all design	20	25
Distinction and/or originality	20	15
Compatibility of all materials	20	20
Perfection of decorative unit(s)	15	20
Conformity to schedule or interpretation, functionalism	15	10
Condition—fastidiousness	10	10
Total	100	100

"Symbols of Progress." An *avant-garde arrangement* in which plant material provides the dominant interest. Some treated material permitted. Background and foreground material may be used.

Pale gray background furnished by committee: 38 inches high, 27 inches wide by 24 inches long, 29 inches from floor.

QUALITIES BEING SCORED	SCORE NO. 1	SCORE NO. 2
Over-all design	30	25
Conformity to schedule or interpretation	10	15
Distinction	20	20
Personal expression	20	20
Compatibility of all elements	15	15
Condition	5	5
Total	100	100

HIGHLIGHTS!

—Judging is an appreciative art.

—It is important to see what we judge and to judge what we see.

—Point scoring is a valuable aid to students, inexperienced judges, and experienced judges.

—Judges should temper their first impressions with subsequent analysis.

—Schedules should be up-to-date and planned for the particular show.

—This chapter deals in specifics. It provides:

   (1) Examples of well-coordinated schedules

   (2) Suggested themes and classes with unlimited possibilities

   (3) The standard system of point scoring

   (4) Point scoring guide—categories and qualities to look for in each of them

   (5) Suggested scales of points highlighting special features.

CHAPTER 4

Phraseology

THE PHRASEOLOGY provided in this chapter is expressive, constructive, informative, descriptive, and brief. Its value is to enable the judge to communicate her understanding and evaluation of flower show exhibits appropriately and discreetly. The words and phrases she selects for her objective and constructive analysis are also of great value to the exhibitor—a potential judge. They aid in expanding the knowledge of her art.

As you will see I have tried to show the importance of the effective use of words and phrases in oral and written comments. When we look for words and phrases to describe what we see and feel, it is best to avoid exaggeration. Rather than choose the most expansive or derogatory terms we should select those that will most accurately picture the degree of correctness, artistry, and beauty of our observations. Remember, too, that it is not always what we say, but how we say it, that leaves the lasting impression. Flippant remarks or those delivered in a sarcastic or belittling tone are in poor taste. The good judge is always kind and constructive.

This chapter is divided into the categories most frequently used in judging flower arrangements. Under each grouping are compiled lists of words and phrases that are thought provoking, effective, and useful in describing the positive and the negative qualities of each category being judged.

You will note that many of the same words and expressions may fit into more than one category, especially if the categories are closely related. As an additional convenience, some of the categories in the chapter are broken down into ways of describing emotional responses and analytical technical appraisals.

DESIGN

OVER-ALL IMPRESSION

Plus Qualities (Attributes)	Minus Qualities (Weaknesses)

EMOTIONAL REACTIONS

IMAGINATIVE: Creative, inspired, exciting, captivating, whimsical, appealing, instinctively well-coordinated; piquant, has a mystique.

Unimaginative, banal, commonplace, uninspired, ordinary, conventional, dull, cold.

IMPRESSIVE: Stunning, striking, dramatic, daring, bold, luxurious, opulent, exotic, adventurous, glamorous, smart, fascinating, aristocratic, imposing, uplifting.

Weak, unexciting, monotonous, innocuous, trivial, trite, static, stiff, severe, lacks diversity.

BEAUTIFUL: Exquisite, graceful, delicate, fragile, fluid, charming, light and airy, nostalgic, sensuous, winsome, alluring, breathtaking, subtle, has artistic unity.

Clumsy, graceless, ungainly, grotesque, overwhelming, overpowering, confused, cluttered.

INDIVIDUAL: Distinctive, unusual, unique, uninhibited, gay, humorous, has éclat, élan, dash, shows artistic maturity, controlled freedom, an interesting interplay of ideas.

Obvious, pedestrian, stilted, inhibited, unimpressive, constricted, vulgar, overstated, in poor taste.

MODERN: Handsome, chic, sophisticated, *au courant,* confident, brilliant, fashionable, new as tomorrow, has sense of style, superbly styled.

Old hat, clichéd, dated, far from new.

ANALYTICAL COMMENTS

ORGANIZATION: Restrained, controlled, cohesive, sharply defined structure, emphasizes simplicity, varied voids, striking silhouette, strong linear design, well-defined linear pattern, integrated, well-developed idea, essential qualities emphasized.

Stilted, angular, mechanical, routine, weak linear pattern, structural outline poorly defined, complicated, confused, cluttered.

THREE-DIMENSIONAL: Varied planes, has a sculptural quality, has dimension and movement.

Flat, absence of variety in planes, lacks three-dimensional quality.

CRAFTSMANSHIP: Beautifully organized, neat, crisp, tailored, effective use of negative space, interesting spatial pattern.

Formless, messy, poorly constructed, uncontrolled, top-heavy, bottom-heavy, busy, cramped, crowded, lacks depth, uninteresting spatial pattern.

INFLUENCES

TRADITIONAL: Classic, Victorian, romantic, Oriental, baroque, rococo, etc.

Overstylized, devoid of period flavor, lacks characteristic features of the era, stuffy, graceless, stilted.

CONTEMPORARY: Fresh approach, new look, current, modern tempo, timely, in the manner of today although frequently reflecting the past through container and style.

Conventional, staid, overly methodical, constricted.

Plus Qualities (Attributes)	Minus Qualities (Weaknesses)

Influences (Continued)

AVANT-GARDE: New concept, new trend, novel, current style, up-to-the-minute features, elimination of all unnecessary detail.

Different only for the sake of being different, not new, overly contrived, unattractively mechanical.

ABSTRACT: Nonrepresentational, creative, nonrealistic expression.

Outlandish, cluttered, overly detailed.

SCALE AND PROPORTION

Plus Qualities (Attributes)	Minus Qualities (Weaknesses)

SCALE (size relationship): Composition properly related to space allotted, comfortable within frame of reference and beautifully attuned to assigned space, satisfying relationship between individual flowers, leaves, etc., individual components compatible in size so that plant material and accessories assume true size, satisfying ratio of components.

Arrangement dwarfed by overly large space, meager or inadequate cushion area chokes buxom composition, arrangement squat, foreshortened, top-heavy, bottom-heavy, massive, bulky, skimpy or thin; disturbing relationship between arrangement and container (abundance of material overpowering small container, limited material insufficient for large container).

PROPORTION (area relationship): Graceful relationship between plant material and container, arrangement in harmony with background; interesting structural proportions throughout, striking, dramatic

Insufficient height for assigned space, too tall for frame of reference, height lacking in variation, height of plant material inadequate, making container dominant.

BEAUTIFULLY POISED *Striking silhouette in green and gold. Dignified treatment of sansevieria and philodendron leaves with gilt cones, lotus pods and sweed gum balls in a crackled Chinese container.* Arranger: the author. *(Photo: William Sevecke)*

effect created through spatial relationships. In sum, all components are compatible in scale and proportion.

In sum, the components are in some way incompatible in scale and proportion.

BALANCE

Plus Qualities (Attributes)	Minus Qualities (Weaknesses)
Secure, stable, restful, sturdy, serene, graceful, poised, has equilibrium, good posture, pleasing symmetry, sense of	Disturbing, shaky, unstable, unsteady, lopsided, one-sided, top-heavy, weighty, bottom-heavy, unwieldy, insecure,

Plus Qualities (Attributes)	Minus Qualities (Weaknesses)
repose based on a solid foundation; complete within itself, visual weight satisfyingly distributed, interest achieved by creative placement.	static, feeble; too exact in distribution, poorly constructed, tending to topple forward or lean backward, equilibrium destroyed by an overpowering pull to one side or the other, similarly extended line on opposite side or a greater weight near axis required for balance.

DOUBLE ENTENTE *Though the exquisite gilt containers are identical, the arrangements are exceedingly individual. Euonymus, candles, lady apples, and grapes adorn the first one at the left. The one on the right is a lush arrangement in delicate hues from peach through apricot to copper: stock gerbera, roses, ranunculus, and euonymus.* Arranger: the author.

RHYTHM

Gentle, smooth, graceful, beautiful, syncopated, rhythmical, delicate, facile, intriguing, buoyant, fluent, easy, flowing, lyrical, sweeping, lively, measured, dynamic, balanced, curvaceous, regular, restrained, lilting, fluid, playful, melodic; easy transitions, flowing movement, graceful flow from line to line, carries eye easily from color to color, from light to dark and from large to small; fluid motion, easy and lyric flow, rhythmic vitality, modern tempo, light and airy touch, lyric grace, appropriate background a stabilizing factor.

Disturbed, choppy, broken, restless, cumbersome, static, ponderous, confined, ungraceful, awkward, conflicting, uneasy, overly methodical, halting, laborious, jumpy, lacks easy, graceful movement; weak linear design impedes rhythmic flow, insufficient rhythmic continuity, lack of gradation causing poor transition in color, texture, and forms, rhythm broken by disproportionate or inappropriate background fabric.

DOMINANCE AND CONTRAST

Plus Qualities (Attributes)

DOMINANCE: Commanding, compelling, important structural feature, executed with authority, controlling influence, leading idea, strong center of interest, emphatic, striking, repetition of similar elements creates emphasis.

Minus Qualities (Weaknesses)

Ineffective, insignificant, weak, lacks punch, contrast, and variety; overdominance or overemphasis discourages unity creating monotony; no unifying element, inadequate center of interest; competing interests divide dominance; too many dominant features destroy unity, too much similarity in line, color, texture, or form creates monotony.

Plus Qualities (Attributes)	Minus Qualities (Weaknesses)
CONTRAST: Variety added by minor discord, dominant qualities unified by slight differences; focal area controlled but gently diffused. *Note:* Lack of focal area or several areas of interest are typically twentieth-century modern. Use of counterpoint and syncopated rhythms are increasingly important.	Disturbing, dissonant, lacks contrast and variety; unity destroyed by too much variety, too many dominant features, too much contrast; questionable or too emphatic focal area; center of interest static, too concentrated.

COLOR

Plus Qualities (Attributes)	Minus Qualities (Weaknesses)

EMOTIONAL REACTIONS

Plus Qualities (Attributes)	Minus Qualities (Weaknesses)
DELICATE: Subdued, cool, quiet, understated, muted, refined, shimmering, pastel, harmonious, fresh, warm, cheery, appealing, charming.	Dull, depressing, unrelated, cold, unappealing, monotonous, spotty, murky, unharmonious, prosaic, bland.
DRAMATIC: Bold, gay, vivid, brilliant, exotic, rich, imaginative, striking, riotous, glowing, joyous, radiant, vibrant, provocative, alive, lively.	Harsh, sharp, glittery, garish, disturbing, unpleasant, overstated, blatant, discordant, over-riotous.

ANALYTICAL COMMENTS

Plus Qualities (Attributes)	Minus Qualities (Weaknesses)
HARMONY: Color scheme exciting, unrelated colors cleverly interwoven, unusual	Color rhythm broken, spotty distribution, choppy, erratic, does not flow, stilted, rhyth-

colors harmoniously combined, revolutionary color play.

mic transition destroyed by divided interest.

VALUES: Color flows smoothly, creates mood, respects "law of areas," * subtle gradations, pleasing variation in hues.

Little or no variation in values, colors, or hues; dominance of intense chroma overpowering, does not observe "law of areas."

BALANCE: Bright hues cleverly diluted by use of grayed tones, subtle results obtained by use of grayed tones and varying admixtures; thematic associations creating harmonious atmosphere, color balance interesting.

Disturbing color balance; color conflict; too much intense hue to balance limited amount of weak color, or vice versa.

EFFECT: Exciting effect in high-key, subtle effect in low-key; color artistically threaded; sophisticated handling, sensitivity in blending and combining, bright colors used effectively against grayed background; striking impression created by elusive, diffused colors, materials colormated, chemically brilliant, exuberantly orchestrated; dramatic, harmonious blend, clever use of unexpected color combinations.

Background color competes with arrangement; color of accessories incompatible with plant material; unimaginative combination of colors; uncontrolled use of colors; overdose of spectrum colors; strident.

* Law of Areas: Small quantities of intense hue balance large fields of weak chroma.

ORIGINALITY AND DISTINCTION

Plus Qualities (Attributes)   **Minus Qualities** (Weaknesses)

ORIGINALITY

Creative, imaginative, inventive, ingenious idea; unusual, unique, individual, brilliant, novel concept; creative artist, nonconformist, expresses self, displays an imaginative force, has inspiring message, emotional warmth, a spirit of individuality, sensitivity and imagination.

Pedestrian, commonplace, repetitive idea; usual, unimaginative, hackneyed, clichéd, ordinary, imitative, mundane, devoid of inspiration, emotional warmth, individuality, inspiration, imagination.

DISTINCTION

Polished, professional, artistic, distinguished, outstanding, superlative, eloquent, elegant, different, unusual, experimental, smart, praiseworthy, masterful, flawless, superb, expert, skillful, utterly simple, careful attention to detail.

Unpolished, disorganized, overdone, crude, overembellished, mechanical, labored, complicated, methodical, laborious, haphazard, mechanics too obvious, distracting from good craftsmanship, too many varied forms disturbing and destroy smartness, unity, and dramatic quality, violates good taste.

Mechanically expert, technically skillful; has flair, a sense of style, restrained simplicity, deftness, dash, dramatic impact, a regal touch, a sense of esthetic unity and design; achieves a high standard of excellence; displays a clever association of idea and technique, an air of restrained

Indifferent organization, careless craftsmanship, lacks style, displays inept technique, is technically correct but unimaginative, fussy, too many gimmicks, undistinguished plant material accessories and background.

luxury; employs gorgeous materials; shows a note of elegance, artistic achievement,
sensitive execution of concept, excellent craftsmanship,
a rare quality of splendor, a
master's touch, inimitable attention to detail, a clever
organization of all elements,
great facility in handling difficult materials.

COMPATIBILITY OF ALL ELEMENTS

Plus Qualities (Attributes)

Companionable, unified, beautifully coordinated, happy together, good textural combination, commendable or
spectacular combination, presentation artistically correlated, cohesive, all components well-organized.

Minus Qualities (Weaknesses)

Materials lack cohesion, no
unifying quality, overmatched,
unity destroyed by too many
appointments and accessories,
aesthetically redundant, in-
consistent accoutrements destroy balance, rhythm, and
unity.

COMPONENTS—SELECTION AND USE

Stylish, sleek, versatile, reflec-
tion of today's fashions, spirit
evident in choice of elements,
good organization of selected
components, diverse elements
harmoniously and cleverly
organized, materials related
subtly, effectively accessor-
ized, elements reflect twen-

Glittery, ornate, overly decorative, busy feeling created by
too many patterns, styles, and
colors, too many diverse elements, texture and spirit incompatible, sharp contrasts
with no unifying element,
linear material too delicate,
too weak or inadequate to

Plus Qualities (Attributes)   **Minus Qualities (Weaknesses)**

Components—Selection and Use (Continued)

tieth century in expression and interpretation, traditional appointments artistically correlated with twentieth-century appointments, happy marriage of old and new, container and plant material appealingly related in color and texture, good tactile quality evidenced; background color and texture enhance floral composition, appointments have a timeless quality, accessories re-echo dominant theme; accessories contribute to atmosphere in scale, color, and texture.

compensate for heavy forms, container overly glossy, accessories undistinguished, inadequate in scale, addition of base might better unify container and pedestal, base demands too much attention because of its size and weight, base lacks weight and substance to compensate for size and weight of container, reverse use of patterned fabric or solid-colored fabric would enhance general effect of arrangement, background too active and demands too much attention; wallpaper, driftwood, and plant material compete, generating conflict; accessories too large in scale, overwhelm rest of setting.

INTERPRETATION OF SCHEDULE, OCCASION, AND FUNCTIONALISM

Plus Qualities (Attributes)   **Minus Qualities (Weaknesses)**

INTERPRETATION

Fresh, authentic, tasteful, lively, subtle, free, true, poetic, daring, inventive, natural, whimsical, nostalgic, sentimental, romantic, entrancing,

Mechanical, vague, obvious, inhibited, tense, weak, pedestrian, hackneyed, old hat, usual, undistinguished, routine, overstated, superficial, artifi-

refreshing, powerful, uninhibited, superbly illustrated, novel presentation, tells story effectively, inspiring message, theme cleverly interpreted, emphasizes motif, deft interpretation, beautifully conceived, expertly told, shows creativity, inspirational quality, clarity of statement, surprise element, understated charm, depicts mood, spirited presentation, clever interplay of ideas, demonstrates versatility, has light touch, flower arrangement and container and spirit well-related to theme, adventurous combinations, classic, avant-garde, up-to-date, fashionable.

cial, ambiguous, unresourceful, hazy.

Modern emphasis, faint echoes of the past, old world elegance with gentle contemporary flair, effective translation of theme, idea beautifully developed, suggests the elusive and the transitory.

Conservative treatment, conventional, repetitive, too heavily garnished, spiritless, shock effect outweighs aesthetic content, overly elaborate attempt at re-creating past, a pastiche, an exaggerated copy.

SCHEDULE CONFORMANCE

Emphasizes theme, highlights occasion, illustrates class beautifully, fulfills specific requisites, conforms to class requirements, strictly adheres

Fails to interpret theme, does not adhere to schedule requirements, disregards class assignment, theme not emphasized, does not abide by speci-

Plus Qualities (Attributes)   **Minus Qualities** (Weaknesses)

Schedule Conformance (Continued)

to schedule rules and regu-   fied rules and regulations, neg-
lations.   lects to conform to schedule.

FUNCTIONALISM (see under TABLE SETTINGS, p. 43)

CONDITION AND FASTIDIOUSNESS

Plus Qualities (Attributes)   **Minus Qualities** (Weaknesses)

PLANT MATERIAL

Immaculate, meticulous, crisp,   Damaged, marred, crushed,
spotless, fresh, hardy, turgid,   faded, dull colored, wilted,
neat, well-groomed, exquisite,   spotted, past prime, weary,
pick of perfection, fragile,   tired, dull, lifeless, weak
delicate, lush, in prime con-   stems, passé, shows flaws,
dition, well ordered, free   traces of insecticide, insect
from blemishes.   damage, disease, poor culture,
                                   leaf torn, lacking in sub-
                                   stance.

EQUIPMENT

Clean, sleek, trim, polished,   Stained, tarnished, spotted,
uncluttered, pristine, place-   finger-marked, dented; ap-
ment of appointments precise,   pointments carelessly placed,
orderly, correct, accoutre-   haphazard, crowded, cluttered,
ments meticulous, linens crisp,   inconvenient, incorrectly set;
crystal sparkling, china gleam-   linens crumpled, faded, soiled,
ing.   wrinkled, unkempt, crushed,
                                   uneven.

TIME-HONORED TREASURES *Antique container, figure and scroll inspire this restrained design of magnolia branches, accented by amaryllis and rex begonia foliage to give it an eternal quality.* Arranger: the author. *(Photo: Boutrelle)*

SCULPTURAL TRANQUILITY   *The exquisite polished walnut driftwood serves as a rhythmic container for the muted echeveria, pussy willows, and dracena leaves.* Arranger: the author. *(Photo: George J. Hirsch)*

TABLE SETTINGS

Plus Qualities (Attributes)	Minus Qualities (Weaknesses)
OVER-ALL IMPRESSION: Visually pleasant, handsomely styled, smartly tailored, table attire charming and well coordinated, excellently correlated in color, texture, and spirit, has the ensemble look; displays contemporary trend, reveals twentieth-century spirit, forward look; spacious and gracious, symbol of today's living, casual look, setting beautifully designed, designs of the past well adapted to modern usage, interesting space areas, varied planes, total ensemble pleasing, inviting, precisely placed accoutrements, new design elements introduced, creative improvisation, unique informality, unpretentious, simplicity with a flair, quiet elegance, intimate style, discriminating selection of all appointments, twentieth-century setting sparingly accented with heirlooms, luxury combined with informality, sense of the past with the savor of now, interesting vertical design, varied heights, restrained use of accessories, distinctive appointments.	Visually disturbing, table attire uncoordinated, no unity in color, texture, and spirit, no dominant elements to indicate either contemporary or traditional setting, appointments inadequate to indicate gracious dining, little organized design, crowded, cluttered, no variation in heights, lackluster appointments, careless placement of accoutrements, ornate, pretentious, lavish, unrestrained use of ornate appointments, equipment undistinguished, overabundance of accessories, lacks twentieth-century dimension.

AN EVENING OF ELEGANCE   *Intended for a holiday or special occasion, this luxurious setting is beautifully coordinated in spirit. Point de Venise refectory panels are placed over a red felt tablecloth. The renaissance gilt candlestick is an exquisite container for the red carnations, rosebuds, and* 'Cedrus atlantica glaucus.' Arranger: Mrs. Edward Ascher. *(Photo: Max Araujo)*

Plus Qualities (Attributes)

DECORATIVE UNIT(S): Unifying catalyst to setting, charming colors artistically related, echoes spirit of appointments, beautifully conceived and executed, in good scale and proportion, displays excellent selection and organization of plant material, expressive linear design, artistic

Minus Qualities (Weaknesses)

Confused, overpowering, too demanding, unbalanced, lacks dominance, monotonous, little variation in color and form, overabundant plant material dominates setting, interferes with service and conversation, plant material unrelated to container or setting, decorative unit inadequate in size,

use of color, dramatic color harmony, distinctive plant material used with restraint.

interest, and importance, unrelated to theme.

CANDLES: Subtle colors charming, coordinated color harmony, adds glamour to setting, interesting placement, height contributes interest to vertical design, size, weight, and style appropriate.

Hues discordant with setting, unpleasant, harsh colors, height disturbing to visual comfort, monotonous placement, too heavy, too thin, too ornate, inappropriate in size, color, style.

FUNCTIONALISM: Appointments and accessories appropriate for specified meal or course, all appointments realistic, logically placed; layout convenient, comfortable spacing, proper size napkins for specified meal, graceful, proper, and comfortable drop of cloth, scale of appointments in keeping with size of table, all equipment compatible in color, texture, and spirit, candles glamorize setting.

Appointments inadequate, sparse, nonfunctional, crowded, impractical, drop of cloth too long, cumbersome, inconveniently placed settings; mats too small, napkins omitted, candles interfere with visual comfort.

TWENTIETH-CENTURY EMPHASIS

Plus Qualities (Attributes)

Minus Qualities (Weaknesses)

PERSONAL EXPRESSION

Great originality, creativity, courage, total impact, utter restraint, clarity of purpose, vitalizing quality, innovator, trend-setting, original concept,

Unimaginative, prosaic, methodical, repetitive, frantic style, weak, ineffective, confused, superficial, obvious or obscure, hackneyed in idea

Plus Qualities (Attributes)

revolutionary ideas, daring, subtle or powerful interpretation of theme, imaginative concept, unusual design, responds to challenge of change, spectacular, challenging approach, strikingly novel, an innovation, pioneer in modern design, venturesome technical choices, fresh, novel, original, current, exhilarating, sophisticated, smart, exquisite personal expression.

Minus Qualities (Weaknesses)

or execution, timid approach, overly contrived, too mechanical, not dramatic, has no emotional appeal, pedestrian, lacks originality.

TODAY'S IMPRESSIONS

Up-to-the-minute, bold forms, striking color, responds to changing times, designed for today, new trend, new mood, new ways of expressing complexities of our time, as new as tomorrow, spirit reveals modern life, jet age characteristic, modern tempo, new twist; pleasing wide open, uneven areas; interesting apertures.

Not up-to-date, lacks contemporary touch, done many times before, not new, reactionary, too reminiscent of the past, tradition bound, slavish adherence to past eras, no variety in space areas, monotonous voids.

ORGANIZATION AND RESULT

Advanced design, flamboyant use of color, utter simplicity, elimination of unnecessary details, forceful linear design, dramatic structural pattern, spatial balance, uncomplicated, experimental, spectacular, startling effect, shock

Done too often, color bland, pretentious rendering, overdone, studied, forms weak, fragmentary, rigid, dreary, dull, staid, prosaic mechanical, hackneyed in idea and execution, contrived, stilted, stiff.

element, element of surprise, components dramatically organized, exaggerated proportions, venturesome choices, technical freedom, strong visual impact, wide expanses of space, clever fusion of ideas, feeling of magnificence, emphasizes negative space positively.

GOOD TASTE

Good taste is doing instinctively the right thing in the right way at the right time. This quality should be reflected in all of the categories listed.

Plus Qualities (Attributes)

EXHIBITS IN GOOD TASTE REFLECT: Grace, elegance, refinement, propriety, correctness, beautiful style, aesthetic discrimination, appropriateness, naturalness, lack of affectation or laboriousness, impeccable taste in selection and organization, admirable restraint in choice and use of materials, a total ensemble look.

Minus Qualities (Weaknesses)

EXHIBITS DEVOID OF GOOD TASTE ARE: Distasteful, frivolous, ostentatious, gaudy, tawdry, vulgar, unrefined, loud, flashy, garish, too bizarre, showy, flaunting, affected, dowdy, coarse, slovenly, unpresentable, aesthetically objectionable, unfashionable, out-of-date, newfangled, fantastic, odd, ridiculous.

INTERMEDIATE REMARKS

More correct than compelling
Methodically correct but lacks emotional warmth
Artistically satisfying but lacks contemporary touch
Good design, though not up-to-date

Good as far as it goes
A good potential unfulfilled
Gap between idea and result
Promising idea poorly executed
Shows considerable courage in approach
An interesting try
Idea had great potential but was not fulfilled technically
Execution commendable, though choice of accessories scarcely
    compatible
Concept interesting, but compromised by too many details
Filled with unrealized good intentions
Creative idea not clearly enunciated

HIGHLIGHTS!

—Hopefully, judges should enrich their power to express themselves orally and in writing.

—Herein is an expressive vocabulary that is constructive, informative, and brief.

—Words and phrases are tabulated according to plus attributes and minus qualities.

—Headings used in the vernacular of flower arranging are provided for easy reference.

—Futher breakdowns are given to describe (1) emotional responses and (2) analytical and technical appraisals.

CHAPTER 5

Put Them All Together

COMMENTS used in flower show judging are generally very brief. They usually point out an outstanding quality or refer to features that have detracted from the success of the exhibit. In flower show schools, on the other hand, comprehensive, detailed comments are required.

Frequently, particularly in flower show schools, the student finds it helpful to put her remarks in separate boxes designated on the judges' sheet. These permit her to emphasize the categories rather than write a complete résumé. This is entirely a matter of choice.

All flower show school students aspiring to become judges know they must take a written examination at the end of each course. In courses where judging and point-scoring are part of the examination, the student's rating is apportioned as follows: 40 per cent is given for correctness of score (five points on either side of the judge's score is accepted as correct and full credit is given) and 60 per cent is given for comments. Familiarity with appropriate words and phrases and ability to write succinct well-written comments will be an important asset to aspiring pupils.

You will see several different presentations of actual official comment and score sheets from specific flower shows. Some groups find one type more convenient than others. If *you* have anything to do with arranging an official comment sheet, be sure to allow ample space for adequate comments for each exhibit.

Here are a few examples of different formats of well-written comments of actual classes used in a point-judging demonstration in several flower show schools:

CLASSES	FORMAT
I	Boxed comments
II	Boxed comments
III	Brief résumés
IV	Brief résumés
V	Crisp phrases
VI	Enlarged résumé
VII	Enlarged résumé

Note: These examples emphasize certain vernacular usages appropriate for judging the different types of classes: Interpretive classes, avant-garde classes, color classes, dining table classes (complete and capsule).

This comment sheet is arranged so that the judges may write in separate boxes designated by characteristics.

CLASS I: AN ARRANGEMENT OF BEAUTY AND DISTINCTION

(To be free standing; staged on a white pedestal, 48 inches from floor; pedestal top 15 inches by 15 inches.)

RULES: Fresh plant material must predominate. (Minimum amount of dried plant material permitted.) Accessories optional.

CHARACTERISTIC BEING SCORED	PERFECT SCORE	JUDGES' SCORE Entry		
		1	2	3
Design	30	27	23	26
Distinction and/or originality	25	23	16	20
Color	15	13	12	13
Compatibility of all materials	20	19	16	18
Condition	10	10	8	10
Total	100	92	75	87

Entry No. 1	Entry No. 2	Entry No. 3
DESIGN: Elegant, charming, restrained. Beautifully organized. Satisfying in scale, proportion and balance. Flowing rhythm slightly interrupted by placement of upper branch of eucalyptus.	Beautiful branch and container present good basic inspiration. Design possibilities not fulfilled. Branch in relation to mass of gladioli not in good scale. Glads are too weighty on left and destroy balance and rhythm.	Impressive composition of beautiful sculptural plant material. Well-organized design, satisfying in scale and proportion. Overly dominant focal area and equally important accessory divide the unity and stop the flow of rhythm through the arrangement.
DISTINCTION AND/OR ORIGINALITY: Distinctive in craftsmanship and in selection of accessory. Clever color blending.	Upper branch has motion and flair in spite of placement. Neither idea nor execution is distinguished.	Materials and idea skillfully organized.

Entry No. 1	Entry No. 2	Entry No. 3
COLOR: Subtle blending of colors adds to both distinction and beauty. An additional anemone of the same tone or material of a darker value would strengthen the left side of the design.	Striking color harmony but lacks variation in the flowering plant material. Container most harmonious.	Colors fresh, crisp, clear, nicely balanced and related.
COMPATIBILITY OF ALL MATERIALS: Unification of all materials, compatible in color, texture, and spirit.	Container pleasing in color and texture, but choice of plant material not particularly harmonious in scale or form. Andromeda busy and not effective. Branch a little light.	Material well related, but lacks textural contrast.
CONDITION: All material in splendid condition.	Magnolia leaves damaged, tips broken.	Condition of all elements excellent.

CLASS II: DESIGN AN INTERESTING COMPOSITION FEATURING AN ANALOGY IN EITHER WARM OR COOL COLORS

RULES: Fresh plant material to be used. A small amount of additional foliage acceptable, providing it does not disturb the color harmony. Accessories, background, and foreground fabric optional. (Space: 36 inches high, 24 inches wide, 20 inches deep; gray-green.)

CHARACTERISTIC BEING SCORED	PERFECT SCORE	JUDGES' SCORE Hon. M.	3rd	2nd
		Entry 1	2	3
Design	30	21	20	25
Color—harmony 15 —use 10	25	20	21	22
Distinction and/or originality	20	14	14	15
Compatibility of all materials	15	12	12	13
Condition	10	8	9	10
Total	100	75	76	85

Entry No. 1	Entry No. 2	Entry No. 3
DESIGN: Beautiful plant material though overall design not well-defined. Maximum effectiveness not achieved because of confused structural lines. Reinforcement and proper placement of main line and more varied voids would produce more interesting silhouette. Focal area disorganized.	Clear-cut composition; strong, smart linear design. Organization of focal area crowded. Size of composition a little small for space. Equilibrium disturbed by visual weight of accessory. Devoid of both rhythm and transition.	Pleasing silhouette. Design is good in scale and proportion. Linear pattern rhythmic but could be strengthened by pruning. Has stability and equilibrium.

Entry No. 1 (Cont'd)	Entry No. 2 (Cont'd)	Entry No. 3 (Cont'd)
COLOR—HARMONY AND USE: Color subtle, conforms to schedule; however, monotonous, lacking a note of contrast. Attention to "law of areas" would result in better color balance and rhythm. Selected background does not enhance arrangement.	Color harmony correct, however colors do not flow easily and lack both rhythm and balance.	Conforms to color requirement. Choice of dark foliage effective against chosen background. Focal area lacks contrast of values and hues.

Entry No. 1	Entry No. 2	Entry No. 3
DISTINCTION AND/OR ORIGINALITY: The reverse side of foliage adds distinctive note. Container simple, good classical lines. Craftsmanship not distinguished, design not original.	Branch dramatic and distinctive, but the rest of the composition unimaginative.	Attractive container. Unusual stand and interesting voids. Dramatic placement of container contributes to distinction.
COMPATIBILITY OF ALL MATERIALS: Materials related in texture and color, but lack variety in sizes and forms.	Materials related in color; background sympathetic in color and texture, but bunching of plant material at base detracts from design. Sameness of textures creates dominance, but without contrast the result is monotonous.	Materials compatible in spirit, texture, and color, but a note of contrast in form and color is needed for dominance and unity.
CONDITION: Background foliage not crisp; begonia leaves wilting.	Plant material fresh and background neat. Container not in good condition.	Materials in excellent condition.

CLASS III: GRACIOUS DINING IN THE CONTEMPORARY MANNER

A Functional Buffet Table Accenting a Past Era or Emphasizing the Present.

RULES: Fresh plant material must be used in floral composition. Minimum service for four. (Table: 30 inches by 60 inches.)

CHARACTERISTIC BEING SCORED	PERFECT SCORE	JUDGES' SCORE		
		Entry 1	2	3
Over-all design	20	16	16	16
Distinction and originality	20	15	16	17
Compatibility of all materials	20	16	17	16
Perfection of centerpiece	15	10	12	12
Conformity to schedule, interpretation and functionalism	15	12	13	14
Condition and fastidiousness	10	8	9	10
Total	100	77	83	85

Detailed comments are required for each entry.

Entry No. 1—Hon. M.

Gay buffet setting in charming seasonal colors, conforms to schedule. Over-all design static, lacks rhythmic placement. Voids could have been more arresting if appointments were grouped. Candlesticks heavy; several different colors of candles disturb the unity. Table covering distinctive in color and texture. All other materials compatible in color, texture, and spirit. Arrangement not well designed, busy. Condition of material not fresh.

Entry No. 2—3rd

Restrained, subtle presentation. Unusual color combination, appointments compatible, but sameness in color and texture with

PLEASANT REPAST *A functional capsule setting. The charming polished cotton cloth, designed in blues and greens, complements the serene arrangement of yucca, ti leaves, limes, green grapes, and cornflowers with chartreuse candle.* Arranger: the author. *(Photo: William Sevecke)*

no contrast is monotonous. Thin branches weaken linear design. Accessories superfluous. Excess foliage at base detracts from design. Choice of color does not portray gracious dining. All materials in prime condition.

Entry No. 3—2nd

Abundant and gracious setting; table slightly crowded with too many appointments cluttering over-all design. Distinguished in concept but overdone. Table appointments appealing and related in texture. Introduction of candles disturbing color note; they do not contribute to design of arrangement. Fantail willow makes eye-catching pattern, but rest of plant material detracts from linear design in color and form. Interpretive presentation is inviting and attractive. All materials and equipment meticulous.

CLASS IV: FASHION DICTATES

An Exhibition Capsule Setting Staged Against a Background.

RULES: Table covering and some appointments for dining must be shown. Designer's choice. Floral composition may include some dried plant material. (Space: 38 inches high, 30 inches wide, 26 inches deep.)

CHARACTERISTIC BEING SCORED	PERFECT SCORE	JUDGES' SCORE		
		Entry 1	2	3
Over-all design	20	16	17	14
Distinction and/or originality	20	15	16	14
Compatibility of all materials	20	15	15	13
Perfection of centerpiece	15	13	14	13
Conformity to schedule, interpretation and functionalism	15	13	14	11
Condition and fastidiousness	10	9	9	8
Total	100	81	85	73

Detailed comments are required for each entry.

Entry No. 1—3rd

Contemporary setting particularly interesting texturally. In good scale and proportion to space allotted. Void at upper left upsets balance. Distinction in unusual plant material and execution. Appointments compatible, other than background and foreground material which breaks rhythm and does not suggest table covering. Berries on napkin and leaf under container superfluous. Design skillfully handled. Schedule nicely interpreted, condition of setting arrangement satisfactory with exception of leaf at base.

Entry No. 2—2nd

Charming, crisp setting in delightful color combination. Choice of appointments heavy in texture and form for delicate, airy arrangement. Choice of plant material and container distinctive. Type of napkins and fold(s) not chic; does not harmonize with cloth or composition. Some residue in container detracts a little from fastidiousness. Plant material and equipment neat and crisp.

Entry No. 3—Hon. M.

Fresh, delicate, pastel plant material highlights this setting. Over-all design weighty on left, as arrangement overbalances appointments and small accessories. Appointments compatible in texture and spirit, but white tablecloth does not enhance or dramatize arrangement. Strong pink napkin and "busy" plate upset the unity and harmony of setting. Condition of plant material fresh. Tablecloth wrinkled, lacks meticulousness.

CLASS V: NEW HORIZONS

An Arrangement in Abstract or Free Style Design.

RULES: Some plant material, either dried or fresh, must be used. (Space: 36 inches wide, 30 inches deep, height unlimited.)

CHARACTERISTIC BEING SCORED	PERFECT SCORE	JUDGES' SCORE		
		Entry 1	2	3
Design	30	20	20	25
Color	20	18	17	17
Distinction	20	15	9	17
Personal expression or originality	20	15	10	18
Condition	10	10	9	10
Total	100	78	65	87

Entry No. 1

3rd, Yellow Ribbon, 78 points

1. Interesting basic design. Plant material lacks strength and boldness necessary for heavy container and for space allotted.
2. Color satisfactory but not dynamic. Background color does not intensify impact of design.
3. Lack of dramatic use of space lessens distinction.
4. Choice of plant materials and design shows some originality.
5. Condition of all elements satisfactory.

Entry No. 2

Hon. M., White Ribbon, 65 points

1. Strong structural design well related to container in color and texture. Base inadequate for composition. Placement of container on base and in relation to background distorts balance, could be improved.
2. Color is pleasing but not striking. Background color choice not effective.
3. This arrangement is a conventional classic design and, as such, does not interpret the schedule. There is some distinction however, in the good relationship of elements.
4. Exhibitor's personal expression is seen in selection of delicate, flowing branch.
5. Back petals of chrysanthemum in poor condition.

Entry No. 3

2nd, Red Ribbon, 87 points

1. Striking concept. Design bold, but not simplified or controlled enough for maximum effectiveness. Driftwood at base in conflict with abstract feeling. Additional height would achieve better and more dramatic proportions.
2. Color scheme pleasing, though background color has little dramatic value.
3. Capable handling of plant material and interesting use of space.

FASHIONED FOR TODAY *A table setting that successfully expresses the contemporary feeling required by Class VI. Smartly styled appointments in tones of copper, wood, green, and brass are re-echoed in the flower arrangement of tangerine carnations, cycas palms, and tritoma.* Arranger: the author. *(Photo: William Allen)*

4. The idea, choice of foliage, and placement show distinction and sensitivity.
5. All elements in prime condition.

CLASS VI: DESIGNED FOR TODAY'S LIVING

A Functional Buffet Table Accenting Spring.

RULES: Fresh plant material required in floral composition. Table supplied by committee: 36 inches by 70 inches.

CHARACTERISTIC BEING SCORED	PERFECT SCORE	JUDGES' SCORE		
		1st Entry *1*	Hon. M. *2*	*3rd* *3*
Over-all design	20	17	13	15
Distinction and/or originality	15	14	8	12
Compatibility of all materials	20	18	15	15
Perfection of centerpiece	20	19	12	12
Conformity to schedule, interpretation and functionalism	15	13	12	11
Condition and fastidiousness	10	10	10	10
Total	100	91	70	75

Entry No. 1

Attractive sophisticated buffet. Coordinated smart appointments
and dramatic flower arrangement highly distinctive. Better grouping
and restrained use of fewer accoutrements would aid artist
in creating more interesting voids, unifying over-all design. Heavy
pottery requires more space. Decorative unit striking and beautifully
executed. Container (crystal bird) and graceful budding branch
are unusual and emphasize schedule theme. Though chrysanthe-
mums are often associated with fall, the springlike budding
branch dominates the picture. Color harmony subtle, though a
little low key for interpretation of spring. All appointments and
plant material show freshness and attention to detail.

Entry No. 2

Pleasant spring setting. Appointments nicely related in color and
texture with exception of the tablecloth, which is too light in value
and too fine in texture compared with harsh quality napkins.
Grouping appointments (i.e., omitting salt and pepper shakers,
placing salad servers in salad bowl) would result in a better balance
and a feeling of spaciousness more in keeping with the theme

"Of Today." Flower arrangement is static and bottom-heavy and linear pattern is not clearly defined. Colors are springlike and appealing but candles are drab and placed too close to the arrangement. Over-all idea is not new, although there is a note of distinction in the crispness of plant material.

Entry No. 3

Inviting modern setting. Appointments associated in color, texture, and spirit. Over-all design is pleasing, though too many appointments too closely placed crowd setting and detract from smartness. Some quality of distinction in coordinated appointments and color scheme. Placement of heavy blue candles and dark blue napkins to one side upsets visual balance. Arrangement in good proportion, but the whole appears overcrowded, weighty, and flat. Pussy willow line inadequate for fully open and tightly grouped gladioli. Arrangement not well crafted, lacks style and imagination. Setting practical and modern, but theme of spring is not accented. All accoutrements meticulous.

CLASS VII: A LITTLE DIFFERENT.

A Smart Exhibition Capsule Setting.

Appointments for dinner—designer's choice. Some dried plant material may be introduced in floral composition.

WHIMSY AND DRAMA *In this example of Class VII, a delightful accessory adds an amusing touch to the otherwise dignified table in green and blue. The refectory runner unifies the setting and the black wrought iron candlesticks provide drama and vertical interest. Arranger: the author. (Photo: William B. Long)*

Rules: Displayed against a background 38 inches high, 32 inches wide, and 26 inches deep.

CHARACTERISTIC BEING SCORED	PERFECT SCORE	JUDGES' SCORE		
		Entry 1	2	3
Over-all design	20	15	18	15
Distinction and/or originality	20	10	18	12
Compatibility of all materials	20	11	17	15
Perfection of centerpiece	20	16	19	16
Conformity to schedule (functionalism)	10	8	10	9
Condition and fastidiousness	10	10	10	10
Total	100	70	92	77

Entry No. 1—HM

Spirit of over-all setting pleasing but not unusual. All appointments in good scale, with exception of swan accessory which, because of its size, affects both scale and balance of the composition. Arrangement crisp and smart and in good proportion to background, but too tall for container. Restraint shown in selection and placement of dried branch and bold forms, which add a note of distinction. Rhythm erratic, poor transition. Eye does not move easily from background through to low accessory. Little compatibility in texture and spirit as china and glassware are too fine for cloth and too traditional for bold colors and modern style. Adheres to schedule, but no new spark shown in choice of appointments or interpretation. Setting and plant material clean-cut and fresh.

Entry No. 2—1st

Startling, unique over-all impression. Design presents interesting use of space. Floral composition well executed, in good scale and proportion to background. Balance and rhythm slightly affected by many small cups. Color harmony dramatic. Smart new accoutrements, compatible and distinctive arrangement and allied appointments present new concepts; however, small squat candles cause spottiness and detract somewhat from design. Setting highlights theme effectively. Arrangement and equipment commendable.

Entry No. 3—3rd

Charming spring setting in pleasing color harmony. Lacks accent or dramatic quality. Scale and proportion of floral composition inadequate for assigned area. Suspended feeling makes dainty arrangement appear even lighter, creating poor balance in contrast to heavy candles. Most appointments compatible in color, texture, and spirit with exception of goblet at left. Moving plate at right would improve both balance and rhythm. Lacks smartness in choice of materials; oft-seen design of arrangement. Some distinction in craftsmanship and subtle coloring. Conforms to schedule but does not underline theme. All appointments show fastidiousness and flower arrangement is crisp and fresh.

BETTER LEFT UNSAID

You might find it hard to believe, but the following comments were taken from some of the examination papers I have corrected. I trust none of them were yours! You can see how incomplete and unkind many of them are. Certain comments should never have been made. Others are merely badly expressed, such as:

"I didn't like the lady's head with the silver and nice plate." (How much better to have commented, "The pottery accessory is incompatible in texture and quality with the beautiful silver and china.)

"I thought the casserole in the middle was too much." (Improved: "The addition of a casserole crowds the setting.")

"Too much junk in the arrangement." (Improved: "Many too many unnecessary and unrelated accessories.")

How would you complete or improve these remarks?

"Her proportion and scale . . ."
"A spirit of material is shown . . ."
"The texture in color is carried out."
"Doesn't put over oomph."
"Trash floating in water."
"This is the type we dread to judge."
"Her club expects blue ribbons and it's difficult to be hard, but
    the balance is poor."
"Not enough relation to unity."
"I feel it doesn't quite come off."
"Focal point too much."
"Needs originality."
"Arrangement has no proportion and scale."

HIGHLIGHTS!

—Select words and phrases that best describe the degree of correctness and artistry of exhibits.
—Remember it is not always what we say, but how we say it. Be
kind. Be constructive.
—Profit through study and review of:
   (1) Examples of well-written comments
   (2) Samples of official comment sheets
   (3) Facsimiles of schedules, classes, scales of points, with
       relevant and cohesive comments.

CHAPTER 6

Actual Judging Experiences

HUMAN frailties may at times cause even the most conscientious and experienced judge to overlook things of importance. This is why the pattern of having at least three judges generally works well. There may be rare occasions, however, when even the most experienced panel fails to observe all the requirements of the schedule and so credits or penalizes the exhibitor unknowingly or unjustly. Such an infrequent omission usually occurs when the judges are under pressure because of limited time or when faced with extremes, i.e., when the exhibits are outstandingly good or highly creative, or when they are very poor. The judge must be able to refer to the class and its requirements; the schedule should list and provide a scale of points. In the class described below one essential category was omitted—there was no category for conformance to schedule or interpretation. In a case of this kind, the class requisite should be considered under one of the specified categories, in order to analyze the assignment fully and fairly. The following describes an actual judging demonstration by three outstanding accredited judges at a flower show school.

CLASS: AN EXPRESSIVE COMPOSITION DEPICTING AN EMOTION

Fresh Plant Material to Predominate.

The exhibit in question was striking and highly distinctive. A massive, uneven chunk of coal was placed on two graduated pieces of gray slate. Crushed gravel was spread on the slate to simulate the earth. One white Easter lily placed tall behind the black coal raised its head in solemn isolation. The background, so well chosen, was a cold, gray, textured fabric. The exhibitor titled her creation "Loneliness."

The interpretation was an excellent portrayal of emptiness and sadness. The design was beautifully restrained and the execution superb. However, one of the requirements in the schedule called for "fresh plant material to predominate." This was entirely overlooked by the three judges who were so impressed by the emotional impact they gave the entry a top award. No mention was made of its nonconformance to schedule. In their enthusiasm, they rated this exhibit a very high 96 points.

The audience of judges and students gasped. They were bewildered and confused. There is a way to avoid this kind of improper appraisal. Had the schedule been read at home and again aloud to the judges before they started to judge, and once more in front of the students at the school when they discussed the exhibit, I am sure at least one of the judges would have been alerted to this requirement.

The judges undoubtedly gave a great deal of thought to the title of the class—"An Expressive Composition Depicting an Emotion" —but they unfortunately did not give due consideration to the other requirement, that fresh plant material was to predominate. A little extra precaution would have prevented the judges from this serious oversight. Although this exhibit was outstanding in conception and technique, since it did not entirely conform to the schedule it should not properly have been awarded a 96. Had this exhibit been disqualified by the classification committee for its nonconformance, there would have been no problem. But since it had not been, it had to be judged. "The Schedule is the law of the show" (National Council of State Garden Clubs, *Handbook for Flower Shows,* pp. 27–39). It guides and governs both exhibitor and judge. When no definite category is assigned to conformance to schedule, the only alternative is to consider it under one or more of the other categories—personal expression, compatibility of all materials, or possibly distinction and/or originality.

It is interesting to note how a second panel of judges, aware of both the demands of the schedule and the beauty of the exhibit, rated it. It was not an easy decision, but it did seem fairer.

CHARACTERISTIC BEING SCORED	PERFECT SCORE	FIRST PANEL'S SCORE	SECOND PANEL'S SCORE
Design	30	28	28
Distinction and/or originality	20	19	17
Personal expression	20	20	18
Compatibility of all materials	20	19	15
Condition	10	10	10
Total	100	96	88

A number of incidents, errors, and omissions contributed to the faulty judgment and analysis in this class:

(1) The schedule committee did not provide a category to cover one of the designated class requirements.
(2) The judges overlooked one requisite.
(3) The exhibitor failed to fulfill the schedule completely.
(4) The classification committee erred in not eliminating the exhibit from competition for failing to conform to schedule.

EXAMPLES OF EXHIBITS FROM A FLOWER SHOW SCHOOL AND OFFICIAL JUDGES' COMMENTS

These four distinguished exhibits are taken from a flower show school. They are accompanied by the professional commentary of the undersigned judges.

CLASS I: A FREE FORM DESIGN IN WHICH PLANT MATERIAL PROVIDES THE DOMINANT INTEREST

RULES: Some treated material permitted. Background and foreground material may be used.

FEATHERLIGHT FANTASY *Delicate willow branches trace a design for this imaginative composition accented by orange lilies in a black, modern ceramic container.* Demonstration Exhibit, Flower Show School. *(Photo: Mrs. Edward H. Bergles)*

Backboards furnished by committee have 1-inch pale gray wood frame. Inside dimensions of frame: 35 inches high, 27½ inches wide. Exhibit to be staged at 24-inch depth on table, covered with dark green cloth, 29 inches from floor.

CHARACTERISTIC BEING SCORED	PERFECT SCORE	OFFICIAL JUDGES' POINT SCORING	
		Entry No. 1	*Entry No. 2*
Design	30	26	28
Color	15	13	14
Distinction	15	13	14
Personal expression	15	14	15
Compatibility of all materials	15	12	13
Condition	10	10	10
Total	100	88	94

Entry No. 1—88 points

DESIGN: Charming, delicate design in pleasing proportion to container and space.

Rhythmic pattern and easy flow of line graceful.

Rhythmic flow would be further dramatized by some pruning of willows.

Light branches not consistent with weight of lilies.

Busy materials detract from design and space relationships.

COLOR: Dramatic choice of background enhances color scheme.

Lilies add dramatic impact to color in composition.

Black container excellent choice.

DISTINCTION: Courageous exhibit in challenging class but lacks force to hold viewer's attention for long.

Effective placement in all respects.

Container, harmony of branch color, and clever placement of bases add to distinction and originality.

PERSONAL EXPRESSION: Sensitive and selective approach to schedule although lacks dramatic emphasis.

Appealing in grace and movement, but not dramatic or strong enough in linear design.

COMPATIBILITY OF ALL MATERIALS: Container and stands well related.

Willow a little light in weight for lilies. All other elements compatible.

CONDITION: All materials crisp and in fresh, clean, attractive condition.

Entry No. 2—94 points

DESIGN: Well-executed design emphasizing modern feeling.

Dramatic design of stylized simplicity in good scale and proportion; has strong linear pattern, with bold forms accenting modern spirit.

Forceful main line pulls too far to side, somewhat disturbing balance; stand a little inadequate.

COLOR: Splendid combination of light and dull colors.

Color harmony smart—low-keyed background most compatible. Base too light in color, making it overprominent.

DISTINCTION: Material well handled and well placed for spatial dramatic effect.

Highly original in concept and distinctive in craftsmanship and choice of container and branch.

Placement of anthuriums distinctive, augmenting exciting impact.

PERSONAL EXPRESSION: Bold and knowledgeable handling of free form design; exhibitor has a seeing eye for effective material. Selection of unusual, exciting branch and clever placement of anthurium reflect feeling for modern free form.

COMPATIBILITY OF ALL MATERIALS: Materials compatible excepting base, which is too decorative in type and feeling, detracting from over-all rhythm and too light in color and attention-demanding in contour.

CONDITION: Superior in all respects; all elements in excellent condition, spotless, crisp.

CLASS II: A COMPOSITION IN A SPLIT COMPLEMENTARY COLOR PLAN

RULES: Plant materials are to be fresh. Background and foreground material may be used.

Backgrounds, furnished by committee, have 1-inch pale gray wood frame. Inside dimensions of frame: 35 inches high, 27½ inches wide. Exhibit to be staged at 24-inch depth on table, covered with dark green cloth, 29 inches from floor.

CHARACTERISTIC BEING SCORED	PERFECT SCORE	OFFICIAL JUDGES' SCORE	
		Entry No. 1	Entry No. 2
Design	30	26	24
Color—harmony 15 —use 10	25	22	21
Distinction and/or originality 20		17	14
Compatibility of all materials or elements	15	13	14
Condition	10	10	10
Total 100		88	83

Entry No. 1—88 points

DESIGN: Over-all impression good; nice feeling of depth; two stands decorative; container not straight on stand.

Grace of snaps does not relate to the rigid line of strelitzia leaves.
Smart contemporary look; good scale and proportion to background; rhythm successful.

Strelitzia leaves large in scale for other plant material; arrangement tall for container.

COLOR: Conforms to chosen color harmony; carnations and snaps well coordinated with pleasing, flowing color rhythm; anemones seem statically placed in color flow.

Lighter value in background and/or foreground would create a more satisfying, more appealing color balance.

DISTINCTION AND/OR ORIGINALITY: Put together with a certain feeling of finesse; has a dramatic force although stiffness of strelitzia foliage detracts from over-all effect.

Use of attractive container contributes to appeal. Distinction in the dramatic colors selected, in the simple, elegant container, and in the striking impact of leaves as well as in the skillful execution.

COMPATIBILITY OF ALL MATERIALS OR ELEMENTS: All plant materials well coordinated in texture, color. However, strelitzia leaves not compatible in spirit. Straight line interferes with rhythm of other plant materials.

CONDITION: Fresh and crisp, except for one anemone which shows signs of wilting.

Entry No. 2—83 points

DESIGN: Rhythmic pattern with interesting three-dimensional effect. Flow of design pleasing and in good proportion to space.

Striking linear design, graceful, seems a little tall for container. Focal area weakened by busy foliage:

COLOR: Conforms to schedule color requirement.

Container well chosen for color harmony.

Distribution of correct colors too even for interest and dramatic impact; a few more flowers of darker value, or a darker background with present arrangement, would create smarter effect.

DISTINCTION AND/OR ORIGINALITY: Quality of distinction in

simplicity and restraint in well-disciplined use of usual materials adds to attractiveness.

Over-all design not unusual.

COMPATIBILITY OF ALL MATERIALS OR ELEMENTS: Materials compatible in color and texture but form of foliage distracting and does not unify design.

Another flower added in the area instead of the "busy" leaves might have had a unifying effect.

CONDITION: Condition of all materials crisp, excellent.

Judges
Mrs. George J. Hirsch
Mrs. Willard L. Fitzpatrick
Mrs. Donald L. Millham

The reader may not entirely agree with all the analyses and decisions. Nevertheless, she will gain an insight into the problems of the Art of Judging.

Every judge tries to be open-minded and is aware of the value of the knowledge that comes with actual judging experiences.

HIGHLIGHTS!

—Do not underestimate the importance of (1) a panel of three judges and (2) specific Scale of Points as a reference guide to schedule and class requisites.

—Samples of actual judging experiences demonstrate the why and how of judging—scoring and appraising.

CHAPTER 7

Judge, Test Thyself!

THE PURPOSE of a flower show is to inspire—to educate—to
give pleasure through growing and using nature's gifts.
Competitive flower shows are educational. We can learn so
much from them. Exhibitors are stimulated and often inspired to
find new ways to express themselves when exhibiting competitively.
New judges have the opportunity to judge with experienced judges,
a value that cannot be underestimated.

We can also all become familiar with new varieties in plant material and outstanding specimens of older varieties—their growth,
culture, and presentation in a flower show. We can learn more
about all phases of conservation and landscape design, so allied to
the art of flower arranging.

In the flower arrangement section, the schedule, classes, and
staging serve as sources of artistic inspiration and beauty.

GOOD SPORTSMANSHIP

Good sportsmanship is like a good sense of humor. It is a gift
greatly to be desired, for it keeps one on balance. Whether we are
award winners or not, we should always exhibit good sportsmanship. We should try to be objective and should conduct ourselves
courteously. It is important to recognize that the judges give un-

stintingly of their time, effort, and knowledge. They do their best. Their constructive criticism should be gratefully accepted. Good sportsmen always gain in the long run, if they are open-minded and receptive. They often learn more from their mistakes than they do from their successes.

Paradoxically it is sometimes more difficult for the exhibitor to be a good sport if she is a winner. One's achievement should, of course, give a feeling of pleasure and a sense of accomplishment. But one should be modest in accepting compliments and generous and kind in recognizing a fellow competitor's creative effort. Accepting criticism graciously and having humility are the hallmarks of good sportsmanship. Competitive flower shows can teach good sportsmanship as well as test it.

JUDGES' ATTITUDES

When invited to judge a show, what should the judge's attitude be? She should:

1 Consider it an honor.
2 Feel a responsibility to the exhibitors to have a knowledge of the subject and a thorough understanding of the schedule.
3 Feel a responsibility to the exhibitors and the public to uphold National Council standards and establish art principles.
4 Have the courage to stand by what she believes to be right.

After the club has invited a judge to participate, what are the customary and basic responsibilities and attitudes of the club to her? The judges' chairman should:

1 Mail the schedule well in advance of the show. This should include classes, time, and place of show.
2 Send follow-up note including explicit directions and/or map and arrival time.

3 Arrange for convenient parking for judges.
4 Extend courtesies of hospitality before and after judging.
5 Have on hand additional copies of the schedule, pencils, and pads. Point scoring sheets are usually provided for flower show schools and larger shows.
6 Never overtax judges by expecting them to judge too many classes. It is physically and mentally tiring. A tired judge cannot give her best. Frequently the last exhibits are decided upon too hastily in order to complete the judges' task within the allotted time. This is unfair both to exhibitors and to judges.
7 Graciously thank the judges at the completion of judging. A written thank you note is a further sign of appreciation and good taste.

What are the responsibilities and requirements of a judge? The judge should:

1 Be prompt.
2 Know her subject.
3 Have facility in expressing herself orally and in writing. Vocabulary should be varied and comments should be brief, constructive, and informative.
4 Be gracious to the committee and other judges.
5 Be willing to understand the intent of the exhibitor.
6 Have respect for opinion of fellow judges.
7 Be flexible.
8 Have the courage of her convictions.

What is the practical approach to judging? The judge should:

1 Appraise the show to set standards in her own mind and estimate the over-all caliber of the entries.
2 Review the schedule. Read each class aloud to other judges before starting to judge.

3   Be sure she understands all requirements and the intent of the schedule chairman, who undoubtedly has conveyed her ideas to the exhibitors. Make note of any questions and if in doubt about requirements confer with the schedule chairman or show chairman.

4   Ascertain from the clerk the number of entries in each class. Count number of entries for accuracy.

5   Study class in reference to schedule. Check exhibits for correctness, noting errors or omissions.

6   Give each exhibit full consideration.

7   Refer to your Scale of Points. Review categories (qualities) in order, without skipping any; then evaluate and score.

8   View exhibits from the front; don't creep behind. *Exceptions:* (a) Table settings to be viewed all around and (b) arrangements that are free-standing.

9   Listen to and respect the opinion of your colleagues, whether you agree or not. Other judges may see things a little differently, and this is all to the good. Working singly, then together, you can alert one another to things that one or more of you may have overlooked or may have been unimpressed with at first. We all can learn; no one knows everything. That is why the opinion and decision of three judges is sensible, sound, and fair.

10 Arrive at your decision. Justify it by constructive comments. Make awards.

A PRACTICE TEST FOR YOU

For purposes of practice, point score and appraise the three accompanying exhibits. Keep in mind that a great deal is lost in color and texture in the translation from the original to a black-and-white photograph.

Use the schedule and scale of points shown below. Then turn to page 76 for the judges' comments and scores.

CLASS: A DRAMATIC COMPOSITION IN THE MODERN MANNER

Fresh plant material to predominate.

JUDGE FOR	TOTAL POINTS ALLOTTED	YOUR SCORE		
		I	II	III

Design
  Scale (7)
  Balance (7)
  Proportion (7)
  Contrast and dominance (5)
  Rhythm (4)
	} . . 30			

Interpretation
  Pictorial expression (15)
  (Adherence to schedule)
  Color (15)
	} 30			

Distinction and originality 15				
Relationship of all elements 15				
Condition of all material 10				
TOTAL 100				

Breaking down this category into its principal elements is a really good, simple idea: an ideal control for appraising qualities under over-all design. Points can be raised or lowered to give appropriate weight to qualities to be emphasized. Other categories can also be divided to aid controlled judging.

MASTER JUDGES' COMMENTS AND SCORES

Exhibit I (First Prize)

Sophisticated, imaginative composition, demonstrates well-organized and controlled design. Graceful proportion and equilibrium is established by height, which equalizes quantity of material at base. (Scale of composition a little inadequate for background space.) Balinese head provides striking emphasis, with contrasts found in

variety of forms, textures, and colors (red, violet-red, orange-red, and values of green) in flowers, fruit, and foliage. Strong forms, distinctive materials skillfully handled produce this dramatic modern expression.

Exhibit II (Second Prize)

Smart, restrained, well-developed design displays originality and creativeness in the selection of plant material and container. Silhouette of sculptured wood establishes rhythmic pattern, which is repeated effectively by the pussy willows. Colors (grayed-green, grayed-violet foliage) are subtle and charming against the walnut wood; however, clear colors of more intense chroma and colors of greater contrast would tend to be more dramatic. More diversified space areas would also add a more modern look. Strong form of elegant echeveria unifies design of this individual arrangement.

Exhibit III (Third Prize)

Impressive arrangement, capably organized; extreme proportion is necessary to compensate for quantity of plant material used. Height also creates dramatic effect; however, it appears to be more than is indicated for the size, weight, and texture of the crystal container. Rhythmic flow slightly impeded by large leaf at the left, which also appears to disturb the balance. (In the actual arrangement, however, the intensity of the red amarylis equalized the visual weight.) The selection of bold forms, varied textures, strong chroma, and emphatic linear structure illustrates the modern manner.

JUDGES' POINT SCORES			
		Exhibit	
	I	*II*	*III*
Design (30)	27	26	26
Interpretation (30)	29	26	27
Distinction (15)	14	13	12
Relationship of all elements (15)	15	15	14
Condition (10)	10	10	10
Total Scores	95	90	89

FACE THE QUESTIONS

QUESTION: How can we break down some of the barriers that make so many of the exhibits in flower shows look alike?
ANSWER: Plan freer, clearer, more inspiring schedules, with fewer restrictions and requirements. Tight, confining schedules often limit originality. Have some noncompetitive classes—exhibitors are more apt to experiment with new and original ideas.

QUESTION: If asked by the chairman of a show to give a Tricolor in a show in which no exhibit merits one, in your opinion, what should you do?
ANSWER: As a judge, be diplomatic but courageous enough to stand firm if you believe no exhibit warrants a Tri-color.

CONTROLLED SPLENDOR *The thrust of the Pandanus creates the movement in this composition, accented by dramatic materials. Anthurium and dieffenbachia foliage, scolopendrium, and red amaryllis in a crystal bowl.* Arranger: the author. *(Photo: William Sevecke)*

QUESTION: When invited to judge a show (not a standard show) that awards money prizes for each class, how would you handle a class that did not merit a first?

ANSWER: Award the money prize to the best in class. Entry card should state: "Judged according to Merit System, not according to National Council Standard System of Judging."

QUESTION: If you were one of the judges, what would you have done in judging the following classes?

CLASS I: AN ANNIVERSARY TABLE

(No other specifications were given.)

DESCRIPTION: The tablecloth was delicate pink organdy; white china, ruby crystal, and accessories were all well-coordinated in color and spirit. The over-all design was charming and imaginative and emphasized the theme. The arrangement composed entirely of pink feathers and tulle was glamorous but a little fussy, reducing the smartness of the arrangement and over-all setting. No plant material of any kind, fresh or dried, was incorporated in the centerpiece. It was the most attractive exhibit in the class by far.

1 Would you have given it a top award?
2 Would you have eliminated it from consideration because of the lack of plant material and given it no award?
3 Would you have questioned the lack of plant material and stated on the entry card, "Not in accordance with Flower Show standards," giving it little recognition?

ANSWER: Number 3 would seem to be the fairest verdict. This exhibit, handsome as it was, did not conform to National Council flower show practices. Even though the class description neglected to say, "Plant material required," it *is* a flower show, and it is essential that plant material be used in the decorative unit. This was an omission on the part of the schedule. Nevertheless, as a judge, I feel that plant material is an implied and essential requisite of a flower show. (Possible exception: an exhibit in a Christmas show.)

Some credit however should be given in a table setting class for successful coordination of appointments—over-all design, distinction and/or originality, even though heavily penalized for the omission of plant material.

The following scores show how two panels of judges differed somewhat in where they placed the emphasis in their appraisal. However the variance is slight and the end results practically coincided.

CHARACTERISTIC BEING SCORED	PERFECT SCORE	JUDGES' SCORES	
		Panel 1	*Panel 2*
Over-all design	25	20	21
Distinction and/or originality	15	11	12
Compatibility of all elements	20	16	16
Conformance to schedule, interpretation and functionalism	15	11	10
Perfection of centerpiece	15	5	0
Condition and fastidiousness	10	7	7
Total	100	70	66

CLASS II: BEAUTY BY CANDLELIGHT

A dinner table set for four, style to be exhibitor's choice.

DESCRIPTION: This setting was beautifully designed. All appointments were elegant and sympathetically related in color, texture, and spirit—though not highly distinguished. The flower arrangement, in excellent scale and proportion, was appealingly harmonious and skillfully executed. No candles were used, thus omitting the dimensions of charm, glamour, and the variety they would have contributed to the vertical design. How would you have scored the above, according to this scale of points?

Over-all design	25
Distinction and/or originality	15
Compatibility of all materials	20
Perfection of centerpiece	15
Interpretation, suitability to occasion	15
Condition and fastidiousness	10
TOTAL	100

ANSWER: Although this exhibit was handsome and fulfilled most of the requirements, it fell short in interpretation because of the absence of candles. It would, therefore, be scored as follows:

Over-all design	24
Distinction and/or originality	11
Compatibility of all materials	19
Perfection of centerpiece	14
Interpretation, conformance to schedule (functionalism)	7
Condition and fastidiousness	10
TOTAL	85

SELF-RATING TEST

Check the following questions in the Yes and No columns. Then turn to page 84 for the correct answers. Total your scores and see how you rate as a flower show judge.

		YES	NO
1	Are you partial to certain colors?		
2	Do you prefer flowers only in profusion (massed bouquets)?		
3	Do you regard the schedule as the law of the show?		
4	Are you sympathetic to the new creative approach in flower arranging?		
5	Do you find a scale of points helpful in evaluating exhibits?		
6	Do you try to understand the exhibitor's intent and give due credit for her effort?		
7	Do you study the schedule in advance of the show?		
8	Do your personal preferences, likes and dislikes, color your decisions?		
9	When judging do you listen to and respect the opinions of other judges, whether you agree or not?		
10	Are you courageous? Do you hold to what you believe is right and fair?		

11 When you are invited to judge, are you always
   prompt? ____ ____

12 Are you able to express yourself lucidly both orally
   and in writing when asked for comments? ____ ____

13 Are your comments constructive and informative? ____ ____

14 Should a judge accept a fee for judging? ____ ____

15 When a club requests a Tri-color, an Award for
   Distinction, and/or an Award of Creativity, would
   you feel obliged to recommend one if you did not
   feel any exhibit merited it? ____ ____

HOW DO YOU RATE?

If you answered all the test questions correctly, you are an excellent, objective judge.

If you answered 12 or more correctly, you are a good judge.

If you answered 8 or more correctly, you are a fair judge, requiring more experience.

If you answered 6 or less correctly, you need more experience. You need to become more objective and to develop a less biased attitude.

HIGHLIGHTS!

—Competitive flower shows are a source of inspiration in artistic, educational, and practical ideas.

—Good sportsmanship contributes to the progress of learning and the joy of camaraderie.

—Important questions and answers every judge will find useful.

—As a judge, how would you appraise and score the two exhibits photographed in this chapter using the given scale of points? Find out how your opinion coincides with that of the official judges.

—More questions and situations a judge must face—can you answer them?

—Are you an alert judge? What would you have done if you were called upon to judge the two classes described in this chapter?

—How do you rate—excellent? good? fair? poor?

JUDGE, TEST THYSELF!

Answers to Self-Rating Test

1—No	6—Yes	11—Yes
2—No	7—Yes	12—Yes
3—Yes	8—No	13—Yes
4—Yes	9—Yes	14—No
5—Yes	10—Yes	15—No

Index